Wandering BEAUTIFUL

a poetry chapbook

CANDACE J. THOMAS

SHADESILK
PRESS

Original Copyright © Candace J. Thomas 2018 SLC, UT
Republished and rebranded 2022

Published by Shadesilk Press
All rights reserved.
Edited by Alyson Grauer
Cover Design by Monika MacFarlane
Ampersands Book Covers

Wandering Beautiful
Library of Congress
2 0 1 8 9 0 8 2 4 7

All rights reserved. This book or any part thereof may not be reproduced in any form whatsoever, whether by graphic, visual, electronic filming, microfilming, tape recording, or any other means, without the prior written permission of Candace J. Thomas, except in the case of brief passages embodied in critical reviews and articles.

BISAC: Poetry, Depression, Wistful, Ethereal, Expressive

To the question without an answer

INTRODUCTION

I'm not one to venture away from well-worn paths, but every once in a while, I take off my shoes and run through the wilder parts, just to experience what the other side offers.

When I first started writing, it was poetry. I did not realize that was what I was writing. I thought poetry had to rhyme and had to follow rules. I was not interested in rules. What I did was journal thoughts and feelings I was experiencing. I started experimenting with my voice here in these tender pages, writing boundless poetry during the fundamental years when I did not know how else to express my emotions. It helped me deal and I found it therapeutic. Some of the best lyrics and heartfelt poems come from these moments of despair and reflection.

I have had many dark days, though not many people would recognize it on the surface. I'm a positive and friendly person who manages perfectly fine in a crowd and on a stage. That does not make me immune to the voices of doubt and self-worth.

Instead of running, I embraced the dark and wrote poetry.

Search for the power to overcome it. Wonder beyond what you see. Get lost in emotions you lock away to find your creative path again.

Search

The Pen

A dream tumbling out of sleep.
One twist...

Raw imagination sparks the paper,
   the delicate indentations press
   the fine details
   of black on white.

The curling script
   circles in perfect rhythm.
Without thinking of movement,
   scrawls a fingerprint
   in ribboning blots.

The tool warms under pressure,
   fueled by creation,
   ignited by beauty and wonders
   unscripted.

Little dreamer,
   eyes bright and wide,
   hold tight and soar.

Shake the Dreaming

Thrust up the sun
And shake the dreaming

Force back the lids
Blink the too bright horizon

Watch the dreams shrivel in its rays
Without the shadows for cover

Cry in an absent pillow
Echo in a void of no one cares

Clench the hunger unobtainable
A gnawing ache for the creative

Scrape the hope from fingernails
Drift back to reality

Unrecognizable once more

Clipped

Bright wings
Yellow, red, gold
Black swirls
Mirrored, but unique
Wonder and beauty
Harmonious rhythm in her flutter
Each wing parting with velvety grace
    And yet, she does not fly

Broad wings
Deep red of November
Feathers brace against wind
High in perches among the leaves
Admiring the flightless colors
The sweet magic in movement
Dancing about, flit and glean;
    And yet, he does not rescue.

Together
    But separate
        Two worlds within one

He could swoop
Dive and rescue
Take her high to meet the clouds
Taste air between her wings

  But he is a bird
      And she is a butterfly

She is attractive and shiny
A thing to admire
   But not to keep

He could snap her with his beak
And ruin the sweet outlines
And traces of her paper lace wings

Together
   But separate
      Two worlds within one

She flits and stumbles
The useless wings
Vibrant and glorious to watch
   But refuse to lift

He stretches his wings
Leaps in the air
Feels the wind
Warmth against his back
He glances a last time

A beauty, a wonder to him
And soars toward the sun.

Together
    But separate
        Two worlds within one

Hidden

Hidden
...Away from daily activities
...Away from business and duty

Safe
...Far from tender eyes
...Far from truth and breath

Secret
...A hunger beyond response
...A need to live beyond the borders

Treasure
... hold an unspeakable bond
... hold to daily dreaming

Hidden
...until the safety net is lifted
...until the chains are unlocked
...until the sun shines on my face

I'll stay hidden.

Seashell

Foreigners
   From a world no person can enter
Formed in an unknown habitat
   By salt and water and waves
Made like bone but soft as muscle
   And live without knowledge of the sun
        Or trees
        Or love
        Or heartache
And then are thrust
            end over end into an unknown world
        they do not know or understand
To be plucked by a predator
   Ruined by a constant peck
   Cast away to roll in a

            continual ...

                  boundless ...

                        tumble ...

Until finally at rest
Someone picks it up
  With a soft, curious hand
      Cleans it of sand
      Admires the damage
      And warms it in her pocket
Memories sealed within the treasure
She will admire forever.

Light

Bring me the light
Hidden under skin
Complicated by life
But shining within

How is the light
Kindled to a flame?
Or understand
From whence it came?

Show a light
Within this one
A spark of wonder
A warming sun

Teach of light
A glowing start
To calm my troubles
Ease my heart

So loving the light
Embrace me fast
My arms are weak
I will not last

Tell me, O light -
Do you have an end?
Show me forever
A comfort, a friend

Solace
For Julia and Wenna

In years past I sought the guidance of a beautiful creature.
Majestic in every form.
Her pure mane of snowdrop white
Fell soft in wind that never knew air.
Her tired horn
twisted with years of wisdom.
Each breath exhaled slowed time
If only to feel the soft escape
Within the perfect lungs.

She led me forward.
The gentle touch of her nose,
The mystic blue color of her eyes
Assured me of my path.
Peace rested inside my soul
And I continued on.
The trail lit by her presence

I come to seek guidance once more.
The patch is overgrown,
Wild and unkempt.
The dust collected in the corners
Of a forgotten shelter.
She is gone,

And I am left alone,

And here my heart aches,
No longer sure of my path,
No longer peace in my soul.
Wind cannot curl,
Time cannot stop,

And I sit alone.
The stream no longer spills its journey.
The leaves no longer play hide and seek.
And one more second is added to time,
Heavy with burden
As it tumbles upon the souls,
Seeking our friend,
Our only solace in grief
That memory cannot erase.

Gone.

And my soul shall seek forever.

All Smiles

Others move, but I stand still as stone.
They come to me
My face is shining,
My eyes light up with smiles
I am the dependable rock
I am the seeded tree

An illusion
The weight of stone
Cripples my soft bones
Worn with time.
My tender heart
Hides behind steel plates

A facade
Chipped away by years of
Pretending.
I am a river pebble
I am a seedling

But I will continue
Smiles become me.

Wound

Sometimes… I speak but do not talk
Sometimes… I feel but do not ask
Sometimes… I dream and do not sleep
  …Sometimes I sing

Sometimes… I cry without tears
Sometimes… I bleed without cuts
Sometimes… I fall without stumbling
  … Sometimes I fly

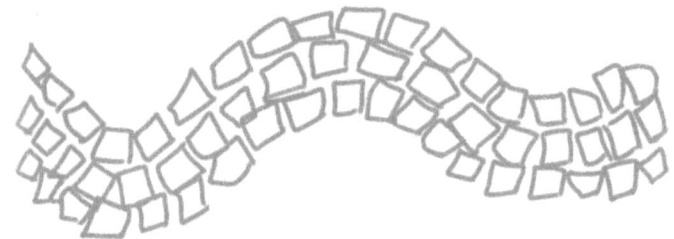

Cobblestone

Broken
Worn smooth
  By time and wars and weather
Tracking the paces
Watching tick and tick
  The smiles and tears and blood
Wash back into the salt in the ocean
Never counted at all.

Marrow

Beneath ordinary skin
 Searing the tough muscle,
  The fibers of every day,
   The veins of breathing,
    The expansion of unconscious motion,
     Passing the brainless function
      Of the automatic condition,
       And hitting again and again
        Against hard bone…
         Lies the scraping, gnawing ache
          Of live-saving…
           Shackled and chained,

      Without the

        …pleasure of

            …..bleeding.

As It Fades

And I look up at stars, and my mind clears,
where everything makes sense.

And then nothing makes sense
And I swim in doubt, reminded of how insignificant I am and how big the world is.
And I drown in stars and suffocate with space and force myself to feel the air between us.
And I watch and stare and search for magic among them.

As tails streak the horizon I look in the wrong place and then catch it just as it fades.
As everything fades.

Wander

And Made of Stars
For Mia

She stands at the edge
She radiates the light
She embraces the world
….and is made of stars

She runs in meadows
With outstretched arms
She captures life
….and is made of stars

She marvels at little things
She harbors warmth
She is tender to life
….and is made of stars

She whispers to wind
She dreams in daylight
She loves beyond reason
….and is made of stars

She stands near the edge
She leaps toward the sky
And bursts into sparkles

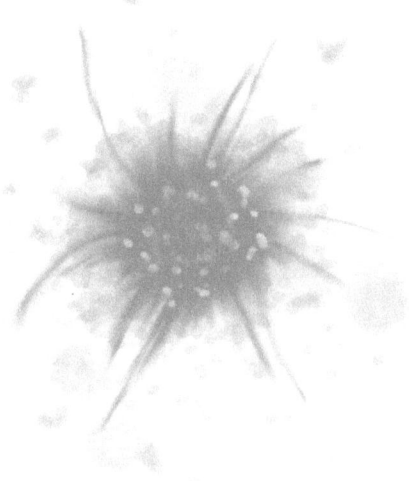

....for she is made of stars

Evidence

I see you...
With eyes that know nothing of how you lived or where you come from.

I hear you...
In wind that whisper of tragedy but contentment.

I know you...
As one who loved the land I love and made it a home.

I feel you...
In the crisp waters, in the gentle thunderstorms, in the brisk nights and tempered mornings.

I want you...
To know of my admiration, my deep soul-sickness full of longing to understand a life so different from my own.

I seek you...
With bright eyes in a dimming world colored with the last streaks from the artist's brush.

I love you...
And embrace the quiet stillness of life so vibrant, so beyond the reserve of simply breathing, a life filled with words never to be recorded.

I see you.

Magpies are Bitches
A True Story

Black and white plumage,
Deceptively pretty,
With green and blue threads like silk,
Floats to my table.

A sharp, steely eye bores into mine.
The gaze reads my nervousness and does not fear.
Maggie, I call her, has no love for me.
Her caw rattles low,
Shaking the table as she lands.

I cover my bagel.
Not this time.
"Shoo!"
With my hands flailing.
"Go away!"

But the stone heart stays perfectly still.
The beady eye scolds me.
Another caw.

I stand.
My hope to scare works a little.
Maggie falters and hops off the table.
Her caw cries out,

A harsh echo resonating in my ear
Down to my bones.

I step forward
One….
Two….

The bird starts.
A small flap,
A caw of fear,
I have her.
A greedy smile covers my face.
A strange, dark satisfaction
Runs through my veins.
A need to win.
"Not this time."

Something high above
Swoops fast.
He finds me vulnerable,
My bagel unprotected.

Piers, the mastermind, tears into the flesh of the bread,
The bare blueberries forced to feel air.

The large chunk grasped tight in his talons,
Crumbs of satisfaction dripping from his beak.

Maggie caws again,
Her last mockery toward me
Before the wind takes her high on the scaffolding,

To share a bagel – my bagel – with her love.

Magpies are bitches.

Diamond Ring

"We meet again," says the sun to the moon.
"The time couldn't come too soon."

The sly smile creeps around her face.
"A different time and different place."

The sun breathes deep and gently sighs,
"So much beauty in your eyes."

The moon turns her bashful cheek.
"The time is fleeting when we two meet."

The sun takes in her flirtatious glance.
"I'll take what time, whatever the chance."

The moon slides and closes the space
The sun holds her in a tight embrace.

The earth marvels at the splendor
A gentle moment, sweet and tender.

Aura displays in darkened light
The chance encounter of day and night.

Gentle words caress his ear.
"I have to go," the moon whispers near.

The sun he knows. "Just one more thing."
He offers her the Diamond Ring.

"Until next time," says the sun.
"A different day, my treasured one."

The moon still blushes in her smile.
"See you again in a little while."

A stolen moment left in tune
Of the secret affair between the sun and the moon.

Language

Words

Like well-known lyrics
  Of a song sung in cradles and dinner tables
  To the young and old
A community rehearsing each stanza
  In their own unique melodious lilt
  The tongue of their ancestors
  Giving the instructions
  The foundation of their lives.

Castle Walls

A hand places a stone and walks away, his fingerprints cemented with the years.

Until a girl from another world touches it and connects with the original mason thousands of years later.

"You've done a beautiful job."

His careful detail on a daily task translates through the steadiness and security it was meant for.

All appreciated with this simple girl's touch.

"All for you, my princess."

Chicago In June

I stare . . .
Down upon a dark world decorated with orange lights.
A grid with impossible patterns,
Patchworked, knitting lives to communities.
At a distance, it sparkles.
The streetlamps play peekaboo through the trees
Tricking my eyes like stars at night,
My first memories.

I watch . . .
The trains whoosh by like a child.
An intensity so exhilarating and splendid.
My eyes race to capture every rooftop,
Every baseball field,
Every heartbeat sitting on the trains.
Contemplating the single purpose
Bringing each here and there.
I observe quietly the interactions,
The solitude among many,
The self-preservation.
We stand together in the brief hesitation of time.

I walk . . .
With spirited stride,
On well-worn stone,
Marveling at beauty old and new,
Treasures remembered.
Monuments of pride,
Raised in times forgotten,
But not lost.
Still standing testament,
A love beyond words,
To a city I just met.

I see . . .
A little flash,
Like a spark to my imagination.
One, two, three appear around me.
I want to snatch each one in a jar or hold them in my hands,
Keep them forever.
They vanish as soon as I reach.
Unobtainable creature of night.
A gentle light,
Gone in a fleeting moment.

I talk . . .
As if no time has passed,
Sharing sweet memories of conversation,
That miles cannot separate.
Wandering like lost children,
Deepening understanding
And strengthening friendship.

I dream . . .
Wildly of a future beyond what I see,
Blessed by lives I do not know.
A future so full of hope
Beginning with such tender promises.
I dream with them.

I am returned . . .
As if I never disappeared at all.

Trapping Light

My favorite time of day

When the Earth is covered in light
That has yet to escape
The sun's disappearance.

I am warmed without the sun.
The light is trapped
For the briefest moment

Trying to find its escape,
Bouncing around every shadow
Until the purple comes from the east
And slowly soothes the frenzy of orange

Chasing it back

To the sunset

Finding shelter in the Celestial

Where it belongs.

Poets with Guitars

...thumping the head
...pounding the ribs
...filling the ears

Singing poets with guitars
Remembering the chords
Influencing a generation
      ...of lawyers, brokers, teachers, scientists
Watching men become boys
      ...and insecure college free thinkers
Finding comfort in a few strums
      ...and impressing girls

Passing through years with poets and guitars

Old Magic

old magic
covered in dust

breathes in the cobwebs
laces the energy of the wise
traps the secrets of the young
cannot wipe clean with a fingertip
ensnares the foolish
feeds on the innocent
burrows deep in the skin

waiting to wake the dreamers

Summer Storm

The prickle of dancing wind
Presses against my form,
Whipping my clothes.
My face kissed by sweet breath
Fresh and warm,
Waking my mind,
Exciting my fingertips,
As the smell of rain sparks my senses,
Lifting my dreams,
Elevating what's possible.
Take me.
I do not fear you.
Strip me raw.
Bleed me. Burn me.
I shall not die,
But become wind,
Existing forever.
Floating on a memory
As powerful as the sun,
Envied by the stars,
Celebrated in the rain.

Lost

Warm and Loud

Lonely, silent conversation
Screams in the cerebral calm
The overwhelming continual hum of noise
Of hundreds of words
Spilling in air
Isolating the one who remains quiet.

Clink and scrape
Slather and chomp
All while the syllables tumble on the plate
But hold the tongue of inedible thoughts
Until the dessert of conversation
Fills each belly but one.
And the room is silent once more.

Wish I Could

I stare and wish I could write

I smile and wish I could laugh

I come and wish I could stay

I stumble and wish I could fly

I listen and wish I could soothe

I reach and wish I could touch

I cry and wish I could feel

I breathe and wish I could live

Blisters

The sun and I are enemies
I am the timid girl wandering closer to the feral cat,
knowing it will scratch.
I am the innocent girl curious about the flickering
flame knowing it will singe.

But I feel we were friends once a long time ago.
Gentle times running in tall grass and scraping knees.

My years of neglect have separated us and he will not
forgive me,
And will scorch me every day
Until…
I am dust.

Lyrics

For Scott Hutchison

Thump and meter drive along
Methodically crafted words
Of the poor, saddened heart
Of which, the pain
In syllables
Prove too much truth
And deem the triumph worthless

But to untrained ears
Brings delicate verse
And hope in every cadence

My unveiled grief
Will continue

A master among poets
A maestro among musicians
Can sleep in quiet peace
While I stand wide awake
Unable to rest

Phoenix

I burn...
In my hands
On my stomach
Down my throat
Around my neck

I feel the damage
In the swelling welts
In the seams of my skin
In the nerves of blind energy
In the radiating blisters
Of my darkest reality

My ache will not go away
My thoughts are never mine

I seethe with my own anger
And drink in my sadness
I wear the blotches apparent
To the honesty
Of how I am undone

I sever my reactions
To the real pain
I play pretend
That I might heal properly
Under truth
Under safety

In arms that will always hold me
And never abuse me

I consume the flame
To be born from ashes
With a freedom to fly
And forgive
And burn no more

One Lonely Marshmallow

Sticking to the inside of my mug;
Clinging to life,
While it watches all it brothers
Melt away in the hot steaming cup below.
It waits…
…as the evil side of me tips the lovely drink in my mouth;
The contents slipping to my stomach, filling my body with warmth and contentment.
I smile at the Marshmallow sacrifice before me.
I relish in the delight of watching the tiny confections melt to nothing.

I wait…
…for that evil side of me comes out with greed
To that lonely marshmallow,
As I flick it down from its security;
Rip it from its solidified cocoon,
Down to the swirling chocolaty hell I have created.

Do I care that in moments it will melt like thousands of others in the very same steaming mug?

Should it matter to me that each little marshmallow corpse lost adds calories to my drink?

No.

I detach all connection to the evil graveyard in my drink
And drain the contents…
Marshmallows and all…

Culture Shock

A blind man saw me as I got on a train.

His deep blue eyes transfixed upon me, his sight between two worlds.
Fear poured inside, filling my empty stomach.
He knows I do not belong.
He saw beyond my skin,
Through the muscle
To the bone,
Roving my catacombs,
Thick with pretend,
Showing flaws flaunted as beauty marks.
The wisdom deep in his pupils uncovered
A timid imposter,
Afraid to lose what she knows and embrace the unknown.

A widow stopped me in the square.

She understood my wild heart,
Combing through insecurities
With tempered grace and gentle freedom.
Magic in her bones,
The whispers of secrets in her blood.
She sees my hollow shell and withering heart,
And pulls the creative tendril tight
Until my heart frees from its binding and remembers to beat.

Collision

Under tender ribs hidden beneath mere flesh
Lies a beating, steady
Unmarred, without understanding beyond beating.
Complete and whole
A machine in magnificence
That without previous interruption
Skipped a beat.
And within this skip
Moves dangerously fast
Colliding into walls never seen before
Blood rushing where it never has
Pressing foundling insecurities
And reopening wounds never properly sealed
Until a beat
Steady
Beyond the push
Surfaces
A rescue to return the reassuring rhythm
To the fragile, tender organ
Of a once confident heart.

Loose Lips

One long thread is pulled
and
slowly the tangle unravels the finely pressed patterned
fabric,
brilliant in design and shape,
coils like a snake to the ground,
the colors mixing layer upon layer as the truth
tumbles on cold stone floor, until the patched hole
lies exposed in the once expertly crafted tapestry.

Plate Spinner

Constantly working
   Keep things light
   Keep things funny
But always revolving
Fidgeting with plates
   Keep the audience entertained
   Keep them dazzled
Eyes on everything
Worried one will slip
   Keep smiling
   Keep pretending
The fate of every plate
Crafting by hand
Creating in heat
Resides with my decisions
My focus
Each unique, each has a story
   Keep them spinning
   Keep them spinning
So the stories won't disappear

The Visitor

A gentle friend visited me tonight.
    His soft rays lit my pillow,
    My thoughts dancing with delight.
Angel wings,
    Like feathery streams bold and bright,
Fell upon me,
    Seeing my worried and lonely plight.
A delicate prayer in my heart
    Sent skyward at the sight
To silent shoulders
Unknowing,
    Sleeping through the night.
Sleep on, in peace,
Cradled with love.
    My thoughts of you come alight.
As I stare upward,
    Brilliant rays of glorious white,
The same moon smiles down,
    On mystical beams by starlight.
Shine on, my sweetest friend,
    Protective arms watch over you tonight.

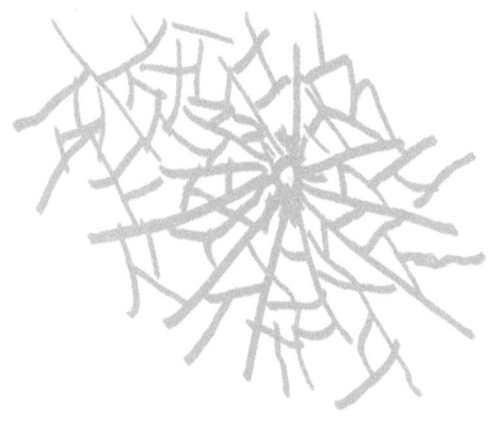

Glass

Glide across the cracks I form
My bare feet sore, exposed, raw and tender from
repeated cuts unwilling to mend
A delicate dance as I hold my breath
Smooth wind lifts and carries
Ever so lightly across the glass
Fearing the slip that will shatter my foundation
… where I will tumble, sliced and bleeding into
unknown darkness

Missed

Your hand slips from mine
Down my palm
until the last touch brushes off my fingertips
The energy of connection
Searching,
Sweeping through my body
A white heat pulses fast
Flooding with the echo of memory
Then disappears
Leaving a reminder
Of how empty my palm remains

If...

If I lose

The world will stop spinning
The sky will forget its color
The sun will not warm

If I hurt

The grass will sting
The wind will whip
The clouds will smother in darkness

If I try

The heart will continue to beat
The blood will quicken
The skin will give to pressure

If I fail

The words will tumble and fall
The meaning will disappear
And the suffering will never go away

Time Thief

Every breath, every brush,
Every conversation.
Every whisper, every glace,
Every sensation,
Every laugh, every wiped tear,
Every crooked smile
Is...

Bottled.
Preserved.
Stolen.
Kept for times of emptiness.
And still wandering
For...

Each breath, each brush,
Each conversation.
Each whisper, each glace,
Each sensation,
Each laugh, each wiped tear,
Each...
...and every crooked smile.

Fair

I am stripped
I am bare
I live new under skin

I am wind
I am air
I travel light and thin

I am sleepless
I am aware
I fear night to begin

I am restless
I prepare
I find solace in my sin

I am creative
I share
I have worlds within

I am shiny
I am rare
I am curious again

I am beauty
I am fair
I tempt the skin

I am hopeful
I don't care
I am close to him

I am fearful
It's not fair
I don't want to lose again

I am dangerous
Do I dare
Should he ever give in?

"Fine."
For Alisha

"Hey, how are you?"

> *I am shattered.*
> *Torn up.*
> *Screaming on the inside.*
> *I am waiting to wake.*
> *I am slowly sliding off the world.*
> *Fog is swallowing me.*
> *My heart won't stop skipping.*
> *I feel gutted.*
> *I bleed internally.*
> *I am drenched in tears.*
> *The shock overwhelms me.*
> *I am underwater.*
> *Life moves in slow motion.*
> *I am completely lost.*
> "I'm fine."

"Do you wanna talk?"

> *Yes....*
> *No....*
> *Talk won't sooth the anger.*
> *I have questions that will never have answers.*
> *I want to know why.*
> *I want to know how I could have helped.*
> *This should have been preventable.*

I should have been there.
I should have asked.
You were there when I needed someone.
When was the last time we talked?
What did I say?
Why didn't you see my message?
Why didn't I see your pain?
Why didn't you reach out?
Why?
Why?
Why?
"No. I'm okay."

"Let me know if you need anything."

I won't.
I don't want to show how much this hurts.
My tears reveal the soreness.
This pain is different, soaked with blame.
The rawness invades the soul.
You can't do anything.
You can't bring my friend back.
I don't know what I need.
But whatever it is, I won't ask you.
"I will. Thanks."

"Do you need a hug?"

….yes….
"No."

"You sure you're okay?"

I am not.
The brightest light has gone out.
The warmest day of sun has grown cold.
And I have to move forward and I can't.
I don't know how.
Each breath hurts.
Gravity is so heavy.
The world I know has changed.
I don't trust anything or anyone.
The waves keep crashing.
How can I love when I'm afraid to lose?
Everything hurts so much.
How will I laugh?
Why is the sun still shining?
How can I stitch myself back together?
I can't recover from this.
I can't process it.
I'm broken.
I miss her so much.

"Fine."

The Boy From the Bottom of the World

And he dreamed beyond sleeping,
...this boy from the bottom of the world,

And caught the whispers of fairy stories,
And brushed lyrics with his fingers,

And mapped skies with different stars,
And marked trails in the moondust,

And played in sun that didn't know shade,
And dark that never understood light,

And swam in sand without beaches,
And lay through months without seasons,

And tamed creatures without boundaries,
And searched the kinder, wildier places,

And drew in air with broken lungs,
And breathed in but never breathed out,

So, he grasped the memories in his hands,
...this boy from the bottom of the world,

And traveled up, and up, and up, into a new sky
...and never looked down.

The End of a Friendship

Am I allowed to grieve
When I cause the sadness
Where my actions
My words
Tip the heart to break?

Am I allowed to wonder
How the world
Stitches itself back together?

Am I allowed to share
When the story is not mine
And the dreaming belongs
To someone else?

Am I allowed to remember
The good times
That out way all the bad times
The laughs, the tears
The awkward and the quiet?

Am I allowed to wander
When the cycle of conversations
Set with the sun
And are hidden from view?

Am I allowed to bandage
Where the scars have not healed
And the bleeding
Is slow to stop?

Am I allowed to cry
When I have what I need
All I could ever want
Without the thorns of pretty roses?

Am I allowed?

Deletion

I stare at words that won't appear.
The naked canvas
Deafened by hollow spaces
Once resting between letters.
The silence blinks.
It rings in my ears,
Steadying my heart
As it finds rhythm in the quiet.

When I close my eyes,
I read them.
The words are there,
Beautiful as they once were.
Delighting... Creative...
An alternate world of my imagination,
Where my dreams reside.

Now...
All is still,
All is blank,
And I stare...
Waiting for words to appear.

Found

Wandering Beautiful

Between the pages
I find your heart
Within the words

Each space is rest between beats
Creating rhythm
In distance

And felt in mutual
Where it finds a pulse
This wandering beautiful heart
Is shared

Dimension

White, crisp sheets
A different sun
Cool feet on warm skin
A new color of blush
Sweet coo of unfamiliar birds
The trail of fingers
Uncovered smiles
Palms pressed together
Sweet jasmine in warm wind
The salt of sweat on quivering lips
Playful clouds
Stories locked within stone
Stolen glances

An alternate dimension

Wayward

A feathery, pink kiss falls upon lovely red petals.
The fairy who lives inside the lonely flower lifts her head to examine the kiss.
It has traveled a great distance,
Over mountains,
Over desert,
And now over ocean—to land on the lonely flower on an island of black rock.
It must have gotten lost, the little fairy thinks.

She flits up to the wind, but there is no current to follow.
She looks across the rock, but no adventurer is seen.
The lonely flower has no other visitor,
No one who cares for the bloom,

The unnatural growth between stone,
The isolated wonder.

The fairy spins around the kiss.
She touches it gently and it shimmers.
Inside, locked tight, is a secret.
A hint of sweet mint still fresh from the sender's lips.
How sad for a wayward kiss to go astray.
There must be a way to find its intended.

The fairy looks underneath and could lightly read the tiniest words to his identity . . .
Wanderer . . .
Shell Seeker . . .
Day Dreamer . . .
The fairy tries to unlock the secret, but it is too strong.
Its magic seals tight, only intended for one person.
The fairy scratches her pointed face.
There must be something she could do.
She presses her cheek to the kiss, feeling the warmth tenderly meant.
Let me help you.

Something stirs inside, something she can almost . . .
The fairy perks up and smells again.
A hint of his scent is placed in a memory,

Wrapped tightly within the secret, too strong to conceal.
The fairy smiles. This clue has undone the mystery.
She knows who it belongs to.
The kiss is not wayward—but late!
There is not much time.
With mighty wings, the fairy lifts the kiss to the wind,
Carrying the treasured secret on her back.

The memory of the wanderer is not lost to her . . .
He explored the rocks.
He found beauty where others could not.
He sought for answers in the storms.
He talked long with the stars.
He swam among dragons.
He wrote of stories too clever for the world.
He carried the ocean with him.

The wind begins to lift, to free the kiss from her shoulder.
The fairy struggles.
No. She cannot lose this.
The secret presses against her back, warm and alive.

Will the kiss ever find him?
A swell of emotion wraps around her and she understands . . .
The kiss has captured her in the journey.

The fairy let her arms free to ride the sky,
The wind caressing her sweet wings, guiding her deliverance,
Together with a secret kiss
For a wayward traveler.

Imaginary Friend

All the adventures you have done with me,
And yet, you are never here.

The suns that have set against your back,
The conversations that we've had but were never heard,
The arguments we never finish,
The stories waiting for an opinion,

All with me…
        Always with me.

Thinking In Poetry

                                    I think in poetry
                          Everything has movement
                                        Motion
             I see things how I would describe them.
          I draw on the imagination of what could be
                        The simple becomes elegant
                  The complicated becomes illustrated
                        Painting words within my eyes
                          Never escaping description
But living in harmony with the poems in my head.

Both Hands

Both my hands
lay on each side
of your face
tracing each tear
and
keeping you locked on me
so you can see
right into my eyes

and

know
the whole story.

Struck By Lightning

A charge ignites
    ...a blinding beauty

A single strike
    ...an ache to touch

A jolt head to toe
    ...a tantalizing consciousness

A force expands my lungs
    ...a moment stops my heart

A burn so hot I blister
    ...a taste of electricity on my tongue

A destructive curiosity
    ...a dangerous sweetness

A soul torn from flesh
    ...a wound free to heal

A suffocating warning
    ...a craving to taste again

Honeybee

Industrious worker.
Lively among a field of sunflowers,
Blue sky heaven, sun gold grass,
Tasting of fresh dewdrops,
Wild, busy,
Gathering as you are,
Carrying precious under your wings
...a life source

Industrious worker.
Walking among a field of sunflowers,
Under blue sky heaven, in sun gold grass,
Breathing crisp country air,
As wild, busy,
Capturing as you are,
Burying deep within your chest
...a reflection

Run

Run
Away from everything
everyone
Run
Then my legs burn from pushing past my limit
The strings snap
The weight buckles
But I run
When every swelling breath consumed with
ache and my lungs cannot exhale but gasp and
wheeze
And I still run
Until an arm can catch me
and bring me back
and hold me until the urge is gone

Timepiece

A Victorian lady
A Regency gentleman
One bows while the other curtsies

Hands nearly touching
An Era divided
Until at the last one braves to find the other
The crossing of two worlds
A grip never to be lost

Surrounding them is TIME
The history of their world
Told within the lives gathered
Each witness the eternal wind to the watch
The ticking begins
The clock is set

Music swirls around the dancers
Uncovering a tale
Revealing to all
A love story beyond the words
The two lovers define this moment

As their beginning
A strike at midnight
A new day
An unfamiliar path

The two wrap arm in arm
And abandon their old selves
Unafraid to write the untold story

Shooting Star

A peer with my naked eye
Into a quiet, polka dot night,
A collected existence,
Calm and vast.
Without warning a flash of light
Streaks in my vision,
Brilliant and more beautiful than anything I had yet seen.

I catch it,
The beaming beauty,
As it burned a trail through the heavens.
I wrap in its glow,
Mesmerized by the spell it weaves.
I long to learn its mysteries
I want to travel the horizons,
To see what it can see.
A moment spanning unnumbered miles.
Its brilliance I could not turn away from,
Seeing only the trailing white
As it led me across the sky.

I seal my wish to you, my star,
A treasure only we two know,

Before you disappear from view.
Star from another world,
Dreamer as I am,
Stay with me a little longer.
Let me remember you forever.

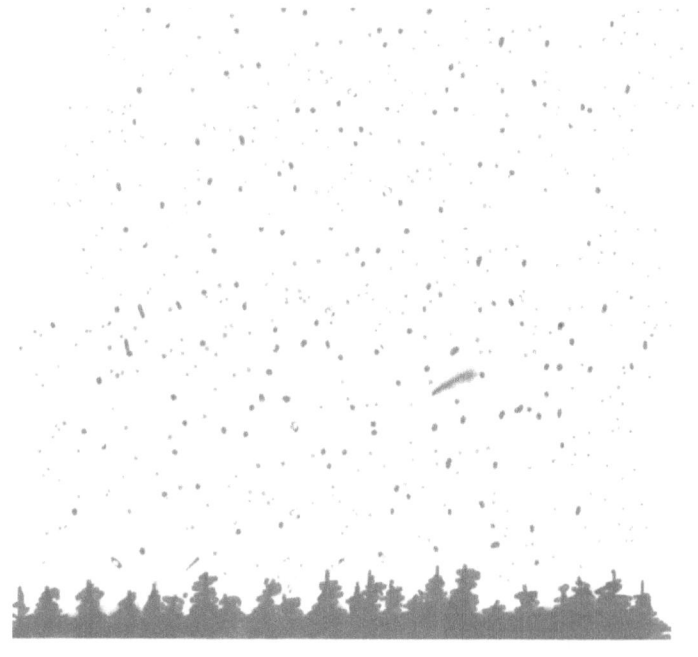

Moving With Tides

Moving with tides
Swell and breathe
A relentless beating
Wave after wave
Wearing my heart smooth
Dark water breaks
Swallowing all that once appeared
And I stand
My arms stretched
Bracing for impact

Scribbles

Scrawling…
        Driveling…
Thoughts…
Nonsense…
Writing words with complex part
        In shoestring letter text art.
With scrabbling…
        And scribbling…
Creation…
        Envisioning…
Worlds without measure,
Depthless and clever,
Conflict and character,
Separate, yet together.
And more sketching,
        And scratches…
        Pile in stashes
        Of consideration in word,
        None seen, none heard.
Just scribbling…
        Driveling… drip!
Words project a world within.
To END is to BEGIN.

Search for light inside

Wonder beyond possibility

Lose your way

Find yourself

CANDACE J. THOMAS was raised by the wild, among the high peaks and winter snow of the Wasatch Mountains.

She is author of the award-winning fantasy, romantic comedy, and several short fictions.

Candace is an ethereal thinker and often stands too close to the fire. She resides in Salt Lake City, Utah where you can find her in a hammock listening to fairy bells.

candacejthomas.com

Facebook.com/candacejthomas.author

Twitter: @cjtwrites

Instagram: @candacejthomas

OTHER BOOKS BY
CANDACE J. THOMAS

Young Adult Fantasy

THE VIVATERA SERIES

Vivatera

Conjectrix

Everstar

Romantic Comedy

Vampire-ish: A Hypochondriac's Tale

To Dream In Daylight

Science Fiction Novella

The Hawkweed

Non-Fiction

Six Simple Steps: Build A World

www.ingramcontent.com/pod-product-compliance
Lightning Source LLC
Chambersburg PA
CBHW030454010526
44118CB00011B/925